Tree-
House
Comix
Proudly
Presents

DOG MAN
LORD OF THE FLEAS

WRITTEN AND ILLUSTRATED BY **DAV PILKEY**

AS GEORGE BEARD AND HAROLD HUTCHINS

WITH COLOR BY JOSE GARIBALDI

KU-534-105

graphix

AN IMPRINT OF

SCHOLASTIC

THANK YOU TO A DEAR FRIEND, RACHEL "RAY RAY" COUN, WHO WAS THERE FROM THE START

Scholastic Children's Books
An imprint of Scholastic Ltd
Euston House, 24 Eversholt Street, London, NW1 1DB, UK
Registered office: Westfield Road, Southam, Warwickshire, CV47 0RA
SCHOLASTIC and associated logos are trademarks and/or
registered trademarks of Scholastic Inc.

First published in the US by Scholastic Ltd, 2018
First published in the UK by Scholastic Ltd, 2019

Copyright © Dav Pilkey, 2018

The right of Dav Pilkey to be identified as the
author and illustrator of this work has been asserted by him.

ISBN 978 1407 19216 1
A CIP catalogue record for this book
is available from the British Library.

All rights reserved.
This book is sold subject to the condition that it shall not,
by way of trade or otherwise, be lent, hired out or otherwise circulated in
any form of binding or cover other than that in which it is published. No
part of this publication may be reproduced, stored in a retrieval system,
or transmitted in any form or by any means (electronic, mechanical,
photocopying, recording or otherwise) without prior
written permission of Scholastic Limited.

Printed in China

MIX
Paper from
responsible sources
FSC® C008047

3 5 7 9 10 8 6 4

This is a work of fiction. Names, characters, places, incidents
and dialogues are products of the author's imagination or are used
fictitiously. Any resemblance to actual people, living or dead,
events or locales is entirely coincidental.

www.scholastic.co.uk

CHAPTERS

DOG MAN
Behind the Epicness!

Panel 1: Yo, Homies, It's George and Harold again! / What up, dogs?

Panel 2:
We're in 5th grade now, which means we're totally mature. / And deep!

Panel 3:
I think I might grow a moustache! / me too!

Panel 4:
SQUEAK SQUEAK SQUEAK

Panel 5:
AWESOME!

Panel 6:
But... our deepness and maturishness comes with a high price tag.

Our new teacher makes us read **CLASSIC LITERATURE!**

Lord of the Flies
William Golding

Fortunately, the books have all been pretty good.

Lord of the

Lord of the

Don't you agree, Harold?

Well, um...

I didn't really finish <u>Lord of the Flies</u>.

WHAT?

But don't worry! I've seen all the movies a bunch of times!!!

ALL **<u>WHAT</u>** movies?

You know: "**my Precious!**"

Well **I** read it, and it inspired me to write a new DOG man novel.

It's a story of savagery...

... a tale of consequences...

...A Profound Look into the constructs of moraLity...

... And one ring to rule them all!

SLAP!

But First, a recap of our story thus Far...

OUR STORY THUS FAR...

by George and Harold

One time there was a cop and a police dog...

...Who got hurt in an explosion.

KA-BLAMMERS

When they got to the hospital, the doctor had Sad news:

Boo Hoo

I'm sorry, but your body is dying.

And your head is dying, too, cop!!!

Rats!!!

But just when everything seemed hopeless, the nurse Lady got an idea.

Let's sew the dog's head onto the cop's body!

OK, nurse Lady!

So they did.

And soon, a new crime-fighting sensation was unleashed.

HOORAY FOR DOG MAN!

Along the way, Dog Man has made some very awesome friends.

Zuzu: world's Greatest Poodle

Sarah Hatoff: world's Greatest reporter

Chief: world's Greatest chief

our Hero

And one supa evil enemy!

WANTED
for being a jerk

PETEY
world's most evilest cat

Recently, Petey tried to clone himself...

I'll make a big, evil villain, just like me!

DNA START

...but instead, he got a tiny, cute kitten who was nothing like him.

Papa!

Li'L Petey: world's Greatest kitty

Li'l Petey's Life Started out Sad...

Free Kitty

...but it wasn't Sad for long.

DoG Man

Free kitty

Now Li'l Petey has a family.

Pat Pat Pat

Kiss Kiss Kiss

80-HD: world's Greatest Robot buddy

And that is a good place to start.

DoG Man

Tree-
House
Comix
Proudly
Presents

Chapter 1

A visit from Kitty Protective Services

DOG
Man

By George and Harold

One morning at Dog Man's house...

Buzz
Buzz
Buzz

clank
cLank
clank

DOG MAN

...Li'L Petey and 80-HD were hard at work.

Buzz
Buzz
Buzz

clank
clank
clank

Well, I'm all done reprogramming the Dogmobile!

Now it's super easy to control!

How's the hydraulic Roof Ramp coming along?

CLAP CLAP

RRRR

RRR

RRRRRR

DOG MAN

AWESOME!!!

Dog Man

CLUNK!

I can't wait until Dog Man sees it!

Grand Ballroom

♪ Ding

Good morning, Dog Man!!!

Look what me and 80-HD did!

We transformed the Grand Ballroom into the coolest clubhouse **EVER!!!**

Us three are going to be in a club, ok?

We'll call ourselves the **SUPA Buddies!**

... And 80-HD will be **Lightning Dude!**

Flop FLiP FLoP FLiP

This is gonna be **sweeeeet!**

OH. It's time for Breakfast!

Cat food and cream for me...

...Dog Food and gravy for you...

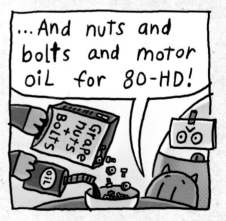

...And nuts and bolts and motor oil for 80-HD!

Grape nuts + Bolts

OiL

STEP 1.
First, place your left hand inside the dotted lines marked "left hand here." Hold the book open FLAT!

STEP 2:
Grasp the right-hand page with your thumb and index finger (inside the dotted lines marked "Right Thumb Here").

STEP 3:
Now quickly flip the right-hand page back and forth until the picture appears to be Animated.

(for extra fun, try adding your own sound-effects!)

O.RAMA

Remember,

while you are Flipping,
be sure you can see
The image on page 23
AND the image on page 25.

If you Flip Quickly,
the two pictures will
starT To Look Like
one **Animated** cartoon!

Don't Forget to
add your own
Sound-effects!

Left
hand here.

Right Thumb here.

That's **BETTER**!!!

I was sent here by Kitty Protective Services...

Apparently, you've got a kitten who should be in **School!**

Come with me, young man!

GRRRRRRRR

Don't you **DARE** Growl at **ME!!!**

I'll go to School...

...and we can play together when I get back, okay?

Bye, Dog Man! Bye, 80-HD!

Hey, where's the School at, Papa?

We're not going to School. We're getting outta town!

Why?

Because you're in terrible **DANGER!**

Why?

I'm not gonna tell you!

Why?

Because every time I tell a story, you always interrupt me, like, a Thousand Times!

Why?

BECAUSE You're A PEST!!!

Why?

SiT DOWN!!!

why?

Because we need to talk!

why?

Look --- it's **very irritating** when you c

Hey Papa, you got weird hairs in your nose!

You Just INTERRU

I won't interrupt anymore. I'll be good.

ALRight, because what I'm about to tell you is

Hey Papa, is this Story gonna be boring?

CHAPTER 2
PETEY'S STORY
(WITH MANY (INTERRUPTIONS))

40

43

But the water rose higher and higher...

...and soon we were washed away.

The storm raged for weeks and weeks.

Finally, we landed on a deserted island.

48

53

60

JUST PAY ATTENTION!

Okay.

So Anyway...

...Then, we're gonna take over the world in our **GIANT ROBO-BRONTOSAURUS!!!**

It's Parked Outside!!!

HAW HAW HAW HAW HAW

HAW HAW HAW HAW HAW

65

So **THAT'S** why I came to get you...

...And **THAT'S** why we need to get as far away from here as possible.

But Papa, if the bad guys got locked up, why are we running?

Because they'll probably **ESCAPE!**

But how could they escape from a maximum security prison?

Who knows? Maybe something **DUMB** will happen!

Chapter 3
Something Dumb Happens!

by George Beard and Harold Hutchins

Meanwhile...

COPS

Ring-Ring

Hello?

chief

Help! There's been a JaiL escape!!!

chief

Where?

at the JaiL.

Oh!

chief

I'll put my best man on it!!!!!!!

chief

Oh, DOG MAN!

chief

Ten Minutes Later

Hello, I'm Sarah Hatoff reporting from Cat Jail...

...where chief and Milly have just caught three crooks!

How'd ya do it?

Well, first they attacked us...

Let's roll the clip...

...iN FLiP-O-RAMA

Left hand here.

Right
Thumb
here.

Things were looking bad for us...

...So we ran to the Jail Library...

...and fought back using the **Power** of **BOOKS!**

Let's BOOK These Bozos!

Encyclopedia Obsoletica

Dictionary

OK, roll the clip!

FLIP-O-RAMA

Left hand here.

Right Thumb here.

Well, congratulations on capturing the crooks!!!

Thanks. I only wish Dog Man was here.

Yeah, where **IS** Dog Man?

I'm gonna find out!

Beep Beep Beep

RuFF
RuFF
RuFF

♪ RiNG-RiNG-RiNG ♪

DOG MAN--- WHere Are You?

Come on, Zuzu! Let's follow them!

DOG MAN, Those Guys escaped because of **YOU!!!**

GO HOME!

But Chief—

Sorry, Milly, He's gotta Learn his Lesson!

...And **We've** gotta catch those crooks Again!

Tree-house Comix Proudly Presents

Chapter 4
Revenge of the Fleas!

by George and Harold

AAAAH!

Papa! You're s'posed to say "a big Robot brontosaurus who?"

This is Sarah Hatoff with a breaking news update!

A big Robot brontosaurus is attacking...

...and the good guys are in hot pursuit!

We should come up with a better name!

Yeah!

IT'S TOO LATE!!! I ALREADY ORDERED COFFEE MUGS AND MOUSE PADS!!!

Besides--- We've got more **IMPORTANT** Things to do!!!

Not if we can help it!!!

FLIP-O-RAMA ★BATTLE★

Left hand here.

Right
Thumb
here.

That's not the point!

The point is, you were expecting someone named "Dwayne."

Cat Jail

But I switched it around!

That's why it's funny!

It woulda been funnier if the bathtub pooped on your head!

WHAT IS IT WITH YOU AND POOP?

Ha Ha Ha

CHAPTER 5

A Buncha Stuff That Happened Next

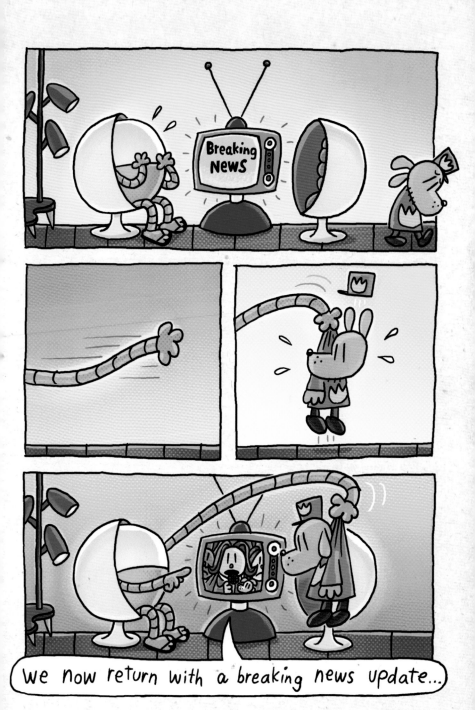

We now return with a breaking news update...

Meanwhile...

Where are we goin', Papa?

We've gotta get out of town! I told you!!!

No, Papa! We gotta go back and save Sarah and Zuzu and Milly and Chief!!!

We **CAN'T!** We don't have any weapons!

All we've got is this measly old Shrink ray! It only has **Two Shots** Left!!!

But Papa—

... Ummm... Atchoo Rebibyablabluh...

ALRight, ALRight! I Get the Point!!!

But if I help your friends, then **You've** gotta do something for **ME!**

What?

Hmmm...

What, Papa?

THAT'S IT!!!

You've gotta stop calling me "Papa."

but why?

Look—we've been through this a MILLION TIMES!

I AM NOT YOUR PAPA!

You're MY CLONE! There's A BIG DIFFERENCE!!!

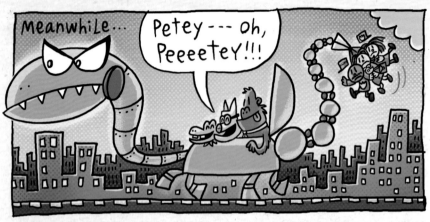

Here's the plan!

You stay here while I sneak out there...

... if I'm lucky, I'll be able to shrink those jerks...

...without hitting your friends!

ahhh...

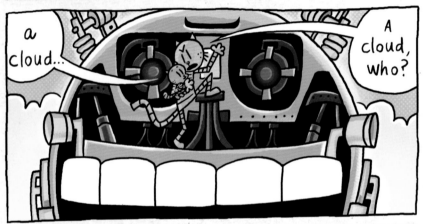

a cloud...

A cloud, who?

A cloud pooped on your nose!

Ha Ha Ha Ha Ha Ha Ha Ha

CHAPTER 6

SUPA BUDDIES

Umm--- What are you guys doing?

DON'T WAVE AT HIM! He's our ENEMY!

And any enemy of **OURS** Shall Soon be **ANNIHILATED!**

What do you have to Say to **THAT?**

Knock-Knock!

135

Who's there?

Ummmm...

a airplane.

An airplane who?

A airplane pooped on your eyebrow!

THAT'S **NOT** FUNNY!!!

We're STILL FALLING!

And I'm about to crash into the ground!!!

PLOOF!

FLUP

Good catch, the Bark Knight!

Well, when you think about it...

None of us existed for trillions of years **BEFORE** we were born...

..And we didn't seem to mind it Then!

Yeah--- I didn't even notice!!!!!

chief

True dat!

Let's not cry 'cuz we're Gonna die. Let's Laugh 'cuz we Got to **Live!!!**

Ha-Ha!

Yeah! Ha-Ha!

FACTORY

HOORAY FOR THE SUPA BUDDIES!

Don't celebrate just yet...

... 'cuz we're BAAAAACK!!!

It took forever, but we finally got our-selves out from under that building!!!

And **NOW**, we're gonna finish you **ALL** off...

...with **ONE ZAP** of our **killer death ray!**

So you'd better say "Goodbye!"

Bye-bye, Dog Man!

So Long, Sarah!

Au revoir, Zuzu!

Adiós, Milly!

We love you, 80-HD!

WOULD YOU GUYS STOP BEING SO PLEASANT ABOUT EVERYTHING?!?

GO ON, ZAP 'em!

ZAP

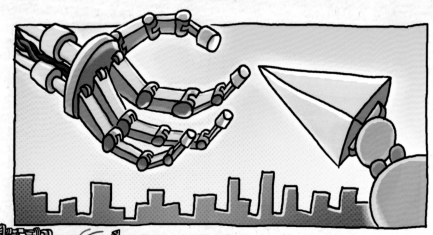

YANK!

Looks like we're gonna have a Giant Robo-Battle...

...iN FLIP-O-RAMA!

Left hand here.

Right
Thumb
here.

I don't know **why** you're helping those guys...

YOU'RE A VILLAIN!

Yeah, I know—but...

...but I'm tryin' to change.

OH, ReeeeEALLY? well How's **THIS** For a change?

FLIP -O- RAMA

Left hand here.

Left hand here.

Right
Thumb
here.

CHAPTER 7
The Darkness

Two hours later...

PETEY!!!

CLONK

We've been battling for **HOURS**...

...And it hasn't gotten us **ANYWHERE!!!**

A Partner in crime?

Isn't that why you Created that dumb Little Kitten in the first place?

Meanwhile...

Everyone was Transfixed by the drama above...

... When Suddenly...

AWESOME!

SWOOOSH

CRASH

Oh, NO!!! Petey's in trouble! Let's GO!!

Well, well, Well...

All of my **Enemies** Are together in **ONE PLACE!** How **CONVENIENT!!!**

OH, **CRUNKY!** OH, **BUB!!!**

CRUNKY! BUB!!!

THIS IS **NOT** A DEMOCRACY!

YOU GUYS DON'T GET TO VOTE!!!

why? why? why?

SLAP

Mean-while...

I—I can't believe you guys saved me!

We're the good guys, Petey!

That's what we do!

But...

...Where's the Kid?

WHERE'S Li'L PeTeY?

I'm up here, playin' with the bad guys!

80-HD!!!

We gotta save Dog Man!!!

Oops! I mean, **Lightning Dude!!!**

We gotta save **The Bark Knight!!!**

DOG MAN--- WAKE UP!!!

The Bad guys Are Coming!!!

Well, well, well... What do we have here?

It looks like you guys got yourselves in a big **MESS!!!**

Do you have any **LAST WORDS** before we **ZAP** you all to **SMiThereens?**

Ummm...

...hmmm...

We'll tell ya our last word in a minute, ok?

OK, Strange flying Cyborg kitten I've never met before. Take whatever you like!

Thanks, Mister Squirty!

ZOOM

Left
hand here.

Right Thumb here.

Love, Sloppily

Right Thumb here.

Love, Sloppily

CHAPTER 8
MY DOG MAN HAS FLEAS!

Well, I guess we— hey, what's that?

What is it, Papa?

It's that Shrink ray I dropped back in chapter five.

Oh, yeah!

I wonder if it still works.

Let's find out!!!

ZAP

AND iT DiDN'T MAKE ANY DiFFERENCE!

chief

Dog Man, I'm gonna go with them, okay?

Don't worry. Chief will walk me home.

scratch
scratch
scratch

G'night everybody! Let's all play again tomorrow!!!

221

PETEY—YOU'RE BACK!

Hey kid, Y'wanna get some gelato with me after I escape tomorrow?

I don't know what gelato is, but okay!

Well, So Long, Petey!

G'night, Chief!

Hey Chief, what's gelato?

It's Like ice cream.

Oh.

sweeeet!

BUT WAIT...

...if you thought our adventure was over...

Dog Man

YOU AIN'T READ <u>NOTHIN' YET!</u>

Right now, George and Harold are busy reading **ANOTHER** old-fashioned book...

The Call of The WILD
Jack London

...getting **AWESOME NEW-FASHIONED ideas...**

... and desperately trying to figure out how to remove permanent marker from their faces before their moms find out!

KEEP SCRUBBING!

I AM!!!

So get ready for the next epic tale...

... of maturishness and deepality!!!

munch munch munch

Trash

Because an all-new DOG Man novel is coming!!!

Tree-House Comix Proudly Presents

DOG MAN
BRAWL of the WILD

If You Like **THRILLS**...

...And you like **LAFFS**...

...And You Like **AWESOMENESS**...

...Then **DOG MAN is GO!**

"Dog Man is Go?" That don't make no sense!

BUT We Like it!!!

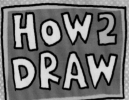

HOW 2 DRAW

The BARK KNIGHT

in **42** Ridiculously easy steps!

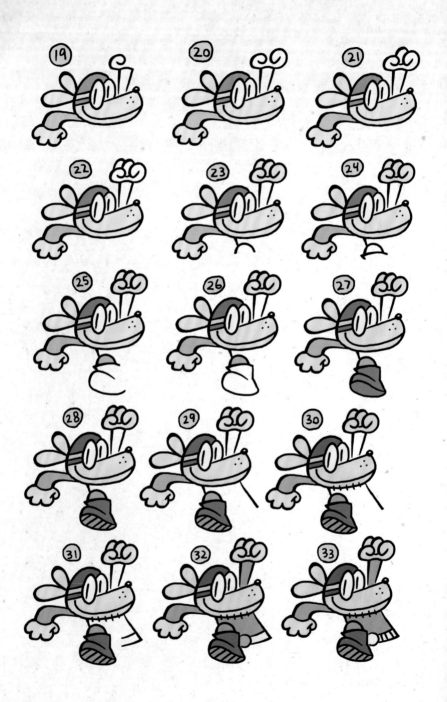

HOW 2 DRAW CAT KID

in 41 Ridiculously easy steps!

234

235

CRUNKY

in **26** Ridiculously easy steps!

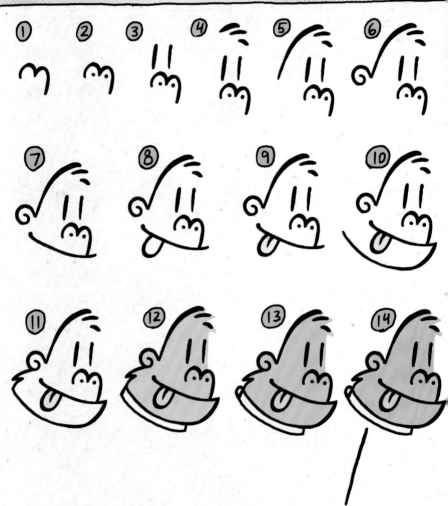

236

LiGHTNiNG DUDE LD

in **31** Ridiculously easy steps!

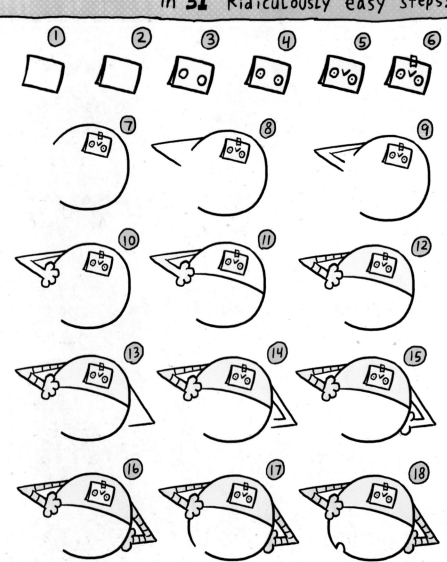

239

① ② ③ ④ ⑤ ⑥ ⑦

⑧ ⑨ ⑩ ⑪ ⑫

⑬ ⑭ ⑮ ⑯ ⑰

⑱ ⑲ ⑳ ㉑

HOW 2 DRAW BUB

in 21 Ridiculously easy steps!

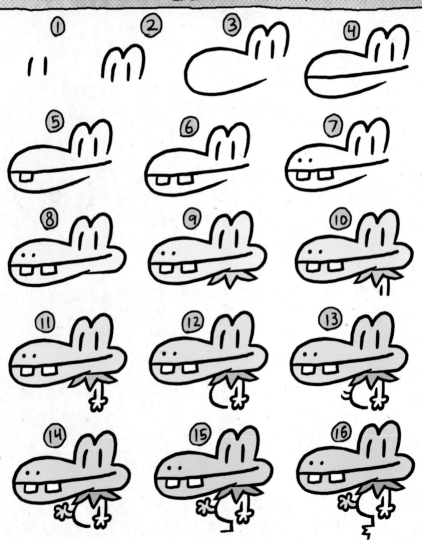

LEARN 2 DRAW MORE STUFF!
at SCHOLASTIC.COM and PILKEY.COM

NOTES

by George and Harold

☆ Our favorite character from William Golding's <u>Lord of the Flies</u> is Piggy. The Piggy in our book is a bad guy, though.

☆ The dialogue on page 147 was inspired by quotes commonly attributed to Mark Twain and Dr. Seuss.

☆ The conversation on pages 220-221 was inspired by the poem "Anyway," by Kent M. Keith. A version of this poem is inscribed on the wall of Mother Teresa's home for children in Calcutta, India.

☆ "I finally finished reading <u>Lord of the Flies</u>. It WAS awesome." — Harold Hutchins

Read to Your CAT, Kid!

The next day...

Jail Phone Rules:
1. Time Limit: 10 minutes.
2. No Hissing.
3. No chewing on cord.

Hey Kid—what's up???

I'm reading to my Dog, man!

Studies*Show that Kids who read out loud to dogs...

...Can improve their skills by up To 30%!

* University of California-Davis: Reading to Rover, 2010

BUT There's MORE!

Because NOW, There's a NEW READING CRAZE That's All the RAGE!!!

It's happening at animal shelters Everywhere!!!

Kids * can show up and reAd to Shelter cats!!!

The Kids get all of the great benefits from reading out loud to cats...

* accompanied by a parent or guardian

... and the cats get the benefits of human interaction and socialization.

This helps make it easier for shelter cats to get adopted!

It's a **Win-Win** for everybody!

Wow! That's a great idea, Papa!

CLICK

2 hours Later...

Cat
Jail

Hey Petey! You've got a visitor!!!

I do?

Hey Kid. What'cha doing here?

I came to read to my cat, Kid!

Really?

check with
your local
animal shelter
and see if you
can volunteer to
**Read To Your
Cat, Kid!**

READING TO YOUR CAT IS ALWAYS A PAWS-ITIVE EXPERIENCE!

SOPHIE & SKIPPY

MAUDE & MAX

MAX & ALEX

MAUDE & ABBY

CHARLIE & PAPOOSA

#ReadToyourcatkid

AARON & PAPOOSA

JAC, KATE & DELILAH

KOUME, RINKA & YUMA

GALEN, FINN & RUCKUS

SOPHIA, ISABELLE, SCOOT & NINJA

LEARN MORE AT
PILKEY.COM!

GET READING WITH RICKY RICOTTA

"A fun introduction to chapter books."
— School Library Journal

"Has all the classic Pilkey hallmarks: comic book panels, superhero action, and Flip-O-Rama." — Booklist

THE CRITICS ARE CRAZY ABOUT UNDERPANTS!

"Pilkey's sharp humor shines, and is as much fun for parents as their young readers." — Parents' Choice Foundation

"So appealing that youngsters won't notice that their vocabulary is stretching." — School Library Journal